Brotha' Do You Mind?

***

by

Charlotte Michele

Bloomington, IN  authorHOUSE® Milton Keynes, UK

AuthorHouse™
1663 Liberty Drive, Suite 200
Bloomington, IN 47403
www.authorhouse.com
Phone: 1-800-839-8640

AuthorHouse™ UK Ltd.
500 Avebury Boulevard
Central Milton Keynes, MK9 2BE
www.authorhouse.co.uk
Phone: 08001974150

First published by AuthorHouse 4/23/2007

ISBN: 978-1-4259-8928-6 (sc)

Printed in the United States of America
Bloomington, Indiana

This book is printed on acid-free paper.

DEDICATION

This book is dedicated to Dorothy "Dottie" McQuinn and my mother Dorothy "Dot" Brown. To "Miss Dorothy" Dottie McQuinn: In the little time that I knew you, you showed me more love and affection than most. You became my family and I will miss you dearly. Throughout a lifetime, I know that you have seen and even learned racism handed down from generations; but you rose above these man-made myths in your life. You met me, you came to know me, but most of all you loved me for me and nothing in return --- there is nothing which feels better.

To my mother, Dorothy M. Brown, it seems as though it were only yesterday that you were here. You taught me more than you will ever know. When you see my friend Dorothy McQuinn, please embrace her and wait for me.

CHAPTER I

Bottom line – for the most part, Black people are fixated on color. Not the color of the beautiful sky or mid evening horizon, not the color of the hues from a moonlit summer's night; but the color of the hues from their kinship's skin. Don't think that it is only the uneducated, lower economic African-Americans because this could not be further from the truth. Being that Black people have been discriminated against for so many years because of their complexion makes it bewildering that we as a race of people would be so prejudiced against ourselves. And that is exactly what we are, we are a prejudiced race of people. The sad thing is that we discriminate against ourselves and then we get mad when other races do it. We are the ones who have made up the names to describe our skin color.

Names like ebony, skillet, coal black, redbone, high yellow, cinnamon, and brown sugar. These names still

1

prevail. I can remember comments such as she's jet black, black as the ace of spades, black as the tire on your car, blue black, etc. One would notice the slang for darker skin is not as "cute" as the name for the lighter skin counterparts. Redbone, yellow, cinnamon brown, paper sack brown, cocoa, etc. do not have the same negative connotations. Children who are raised hearing these names for their darker skin, can but only be dismayed and feel dejected and rejected in their cultural society and the society at large.

Is it the indoctrination into a majority that has for so many decades decided what was beauty. Could the power of slavery still exist today whereby the light-skinned "negroes" from the big house are conditioned to believe they are better than the "field negroes" in the cotton fields? Dr. Martin Luther King tried to instill a movement to reverse this age old atrocity. He began the Black is Beautiful movement motivated more by a more militant view from Malcolm X and other leaders. It was going strong in the 60s with natural hair dos and the darker skinned Blacks feeling for once superior by their deep, dark, rich skinned tones. Dark skinned women revered as beautiful, exotic queens with curvaceous figures and well-defined facial features. Their full lips that others now so desperately try to emulate were finally seen as beautiful. The broadness and curves of their noses now seen as exotic and afro-eccentric. Commercials and movie stars which depicted the single side of beauty being the Euro-American ancestry took a back seat in the new found African-American culture. And African-American men appeared to be proud of and awakened to the beauty of the Black princess.

But, it all came to a screeching halt and we returned back to the days of Cab Calloway. Back to the time when the starlets in the cabarets and movies of African-Americans preferred the lighter skinned "Blacks". Back to the days when certain clubs required the entrance eligibility of the "Black" woman to be the color of a paper sack. And then up to the times where most beauty queens on all Black campuses were very light-skinned African-American women. And continuing up into the times where most rappers prefer light skinned African-American women on their videos and little, dark skin girls believe they are not beautiful.

For generations, our own families have favored the lighter skinned relatives. Preferential treatment to the light skinned children in families has not been lost. It continues today. It is beyond what caucasians do when they gloat over the blond hair and blue eyes of a baby being born. Every race has something that they are intrigued by and hold to a certain standard, but the Euro American culture does not destroy the souls and hopes of their brunettes or less fair Caucasians holding some ethnicity from other dark-haired races. The souls and hopes of little, dark-skinned children are often times thwarted. As a guidance counselor in a predominantly African-American school, when I hear a young, African-American girl in a middle school say, "Black boys don't like dark-skinned girls," my heart bleeds. She looks over at a dark-skinned boy and asks him, "Hey, boys don't like dark skinned girls do they?" He, 13 years old, draws up his dark face with a frown and says emphatically, "No!" And when she further comments, "All light-skinned people are pretty", I look into her pretty dark, Hershey-smooth face she tries so hard to deny and I feel it is impossible to change these perceptions. They continue to grow even in this generation now out of the 1900s and into 2000. She insists she is not a dark skinned girl which suggests she blocks out who she is when she looks into her reflection of her bathroom mirror. But, surely when she watches the videos of BET, she can truly believe that "Black boys", **however Black they may be**, do not like dark-skin girls.

Movies from the era of those such as Dorothy Dandridge or Lena Horne always had lighter skinned actresses and chorus line women. One could try to understand the mentality of a time when our country had made Black a very unpopular thing to be, but we have shed blood and tears to eradicate this neo nazi mentality. The Black is beautiful movement moved out the window and once again, in 2006, the chorus line women of color is still based on beauty without pigment. Come on brothas!

The children today who have these antiquated ideas of beauty will soon be parents and grandparents handing down their thoughts and beliefs to another generation – dark is ugly, dark is dumb. The ooing and awing over the grandchildren whose skin is fairer, whose hair is straighter, and whose features are finer and whose eyes are lighter will continue probably into infinity.

Listening to an "educated"collegue, who happens to be a light complexioned individual, talk about her son being in the sun too long because he is already Black enough makes me quiver. But what makes me quiver more is he hears it. And then I quiver a little more when I see the face of her dark-skinned daughter who could be a budding model Iman. Beautiful features, beautiful figure encapsulated in a dark-skinned body, which she is reminded, in her own home that this darkness is a negative. A mother who marvels at her light complexion and makes comments about how lucky she is to have light skin and light eyes. I look into her face and I want to show the little dark skin girl the reality--- all light skin people are definitely **not** pretty.

CHAPTER II

Dark skinned men do suffer racism and oppression to this date, but once they step up on the socioeconomic ladder and they become physicians, lawyers, famous athletes pro or college, actors, etc the darkness of the complexion holds little relevance. In fact, in the male, it is admired. I have often heard African-American women marvel at the deep complexion of a "Wesley Snipes". Many of my friends will tell me that they prefer dark skin men because they seem more masculine and they are sexier. Vivica Foxx's boyfriend , the well known rapper "50 Cent" makes many African American women swoon and sweat wishing they could only be worthy to touch his broad, muscular body. His well-defined African-American features. His broad nose, his full lips captivate many Black women. Many of my friends swooned over Wesley Snipes in his "hay day" of action- packed films. You never hear this adoration of dark skinned women. A young African-American male can have hope, not that he can become a rapper or an athlete, but that his features and his color will not necessarily be a handicap. Working with a population of about 850 children, 98% being African-Americans, I have yet to hear a young, black male say, "girls don't like dark-skinned boys." We continually condition ourselves. It is perpetual, it is perpetual.

Black men, African-American men, requests that we live up to the standards of Euro-American beauty. Those with lighter skin, or finer features, straighter hair are the object of their attention. However, this can all be down played at the onset of a white woman. For example, I was outside of a club one night with a friend who was bouncing. This was a predominantly Black club, a club most would call "thugged-out". There were a couple of pretty Black women standing at the entrance. A group of Black bouncers were standing several feet away from these women. They had observed the women and made a few comments. Suddenly a "beaten down" vehicle appeared with two white women in it. The Black bouncers, not the White bouncers working with them, started yelling and hooping and hollering, "y'all come back, hey don't leave." They couldn't even see what the women looked like other than they were white females at a Black club. When they did get out of the car, they were very unattractive and over weight women. The bouncers did not say anything else to them. Little Black girls who think little Black boys don't like dark skinned women, grow up to be Black women with quite a bit of confusion.

Although people may consider me a light skin woman, I am a Black woman who dealt with confusion as a young, Black girl. I can only but imagine how my dark-skin counterparts may have felt growing up from early childhood through the teen years. I can remember after returning from overseas with my Air Force dad, how much emphasis was placed on Black people with light complexions, "fine" hair, light eyes, or chiseled features by other Black people. You got some "props" if you had one or the other, but have all four and you were elite in the eyes of those with color. Seeing Black people's preference and admiration of these features hurt and confuse a young mind. Being in high school and having boys like you only to pass on to some one a little lighter or someone with hair a little finer, or features a little smaller could plummet self-esteem.

Dating a light-skin boy in high school once who came from a family of predominantly light skin people, I can remember a girl in a blue jean store where my boyfriend and I worked. She liked my boyfriend and she would do sneaky things behind my back to get his attention. I was telling his grandmother about it one day while I was visiting. To my confusion, his grandmother asked me if the girl was dark skin. Coincidentally she **happened** to be a dark skin girl. His grandmother happened to be a light skinned "mulatto" type woman. She said to me, "You have to watch those dark skin girls." She further added, "They are evil." I was surprised at her words and even at the age of 19, I knew she was ignorant. I couldn't even be mad at the girl anymore. I was thinking, she really makes me mad, but the color of her skin has nothing to do with anything. How can I persecute her for that. I am mad because she wants my boyfriend, she can't help and why should she help the color of her skin. Surely my boyfriend's grandmother was a part of racism when Black people could not drink from the water fountains unless designated "colored." Surely she was around to hear of or see Black people getting lynched solely because they were Black. How could she make this type of comment in reference to someone of her own race she did not know! Looking at me, she did not think my mother could be dark and had no idea how much that offended me and stayed on mind. It stayed on my young mind only to think how confusing --- Black people don't like Black people! I am sure this woman has long been departed from this lifetime, but the sad thing is many people along time from departing still think this way. Brotha' Do You Mind, but this is where so much of my confusion comes in. How do I understand that you want me to be loyal to my race and forsake all other races, when you do not even honor your race. Some of you are saying that I am simple minded and that all Black people are not this way, but we dominate racism amongst the war against African-Americans. Like I tell my students at the middle school where I work, we do not have to wait for other races to annihilate us or eradicate us, we can do it all by ourselves.

Again, I have noticed that dark-skinned Black men are, for the most part, not discriminated against by Black women, light or dark. A good looking dark skinned Black man and even a not so good looking dark skinned Black man can be seen with a good looking Black woman rather she is light or dark. Look at some of the unattractive rappers in the videos with beautiful women, they could get some of those women even if they were not rich. I have rarely heard Black women talking about men in terms of a fine redbone or a good looking high yellow dude. We may describe him by color for only identification purposes, but that is usually it. Even those who would be uneducated or from lower socioeconomic places do not even speak such silliness. When it comes to the opposite sex and relationships, Black men seem to have the monopoly on being choosey in regards to color, hues, and hair texture.

It was such a surprise when I became older, a teenager, probably about 15 or 16 years old. My mother shared with me her plight of marrying into a family of light-skinned African-Americans. My dad's mother was, if you will, paper sack brown and my grandfather was "pretty bright" too. So, naturally, their four sons had light complexions. All four brothers, including my father, married women, who for lack of a better term would be considered "mulatto". My father and his first wife produced two very light-skinned children with "fine" curly hair. Time would pass and my father and his wife divorced as he found out she was sleeping with other men while he was away with the military. My father met my mother in a small town in Panama City, Florida. To the point --- my mother was a dark skinned, young woman. She was totally the opposite of his first wife. He married what he thought he was supposed to the first time, but my dad was strong willed and has always done it his way. Mom was a beautiful, stunning young woman. She had beautiful features with high cheek bones, big, brown eyes and a coca cola bottled figure to die for. He met her when she was 17 years old. He fell madly in love with her and was in love and obsessed with her until he died at the age of 59, 11 years later, she died at the age of 59 as well. I will always love my dad "hard" for seeing my mother's dark beauty in a world of "colored" people who did not see her worth. Without his seeing her worth, I would not be typing these words.

The way my mother described meeting my father's family reminded me of "Guess Who's Coming to Dinner" with Sidney Poitier. It was like my father was bringing this Black woman to a "well to do" white family. They were a lower-middle class family who had more status because of their light complexions. I guess in the Black world of the 30s, 40s, and 50s, they were more upper class amongst Blacks, because of their complexions. They did not even scale amongst White America. This is why Black racism, Black on Black degradation is so confusing for me. I am full of anger because of how Black people treat each other.

My grandmother was a nurse or more probable a nurse's aid and my grandfather was of all things, a preacher. He was a preacher, not a pastor. There was nothing pastoral about him. He was mean to his kids and beat his wife. Nevertheless, my dad's parents were not pleased with his dark skinned beauty. My mother and father got married without their knowledge while she carried a soon to be beautiful darker-skinned baby boy. They accepted it; but did not appreciate it. And I always noticed the difference in how my grandparents treated me and how they treated my beautiful, darker-brown-skinned brother.

My father was the brother that did not care about what others thought and he was not going to let his parents influence his life decisions. The other brothers would have never been so bold. My mother told me stories of how the other wives treated her and the derogatory comments they would all make. There was one wife that did embrace my mother and they became friends. Luckily for mom, there was very little time spent around these people because my father was in the Air Force and they spent most time visiting before moving overseas or to some other state. But those times when she was there, she and my Uncle Tommy's wife Liz became close. Liz was Black, I think. I was never really sure. She had the "mulatto" complexion with jet black, shiny, wavy hair. She almost looked Spanish. She had a very slender frame and she was very pretty and adorned her hands with long, beautifully painted nails. Liz was an excellent singer on the scale of a Minnie Ripperton. She was so talented she actually made several albums and debuted on one of Bob Hope's specials, but she had a drinking and drug problem which cost her dearly. She told my mother how her new in-laws had made the comment, "why did DeeDee (my father's nickname) bring that dark girl here?" These are the same people that were unable to drink from water fountains unless they were for the "colored". These were the same people who lived in a time when they actually saw men lynched for the color of their skin. These were the same people who could not be admitted in the front door of some establishments because they, no matter how "light" or near white they may have looked they were still Black. They had the audacity to detest Blackness. Another comment made was, "Dot looks pretty from the back because you can't see how dark she is." "She's dark, but she has a nice shape." As for grandchildren, there was my brother and I. I was the lighter of the two of us and I could always feel the preferential treatment that I received. I loved my brother –this was unfair and it hurt me. I always hoped he did not notice the difference in how we were treated.

Once my brother and I were teasing and playing a game in which we pointed out our differences. I was about six and he was about nine years old. He would say something like, "My hands are bigger than yours," and I would retort, "My hair is longer than yours" and so on. Well, not knowing that my mother was listening in the other bedroom and not caring because we were merely playing an innocent, silly game, I stated in fun, "My skin is lighter than yours," or I may have said, "Your skin is darker than mine." So many years ago I can not remember the exact order of words, but what stung in my mind for a lifetime was how angry my mother was when she whipped around the doorway of that room.

She got in my six year old face and said, "Don't you ever let me hear you say that again!" It hurt my feelings so much that I remember it to this very day. I truly didn't understand her wrath. Color consciousness as we know it was obsolete in my life. We lived in Okinawa, on the economy surrounded by Okinawans and rarely came into contact with our own race. In my Kindergarten I can't even remember if there was another Black child in my classroom. But later, understanding the prejudice and racism my mother experienced, not only outside of her race, but within; the pain from her disappointment in me lessened a little. I felt sad as if I had somehow hurt my brother and neither of us knew why. He sensed from her behavior I had done something wrong to him and I felt guilty for it for years.

My mother told me of another time which would be impossible for me to remember because I was a toddler just learning how to walk and unfortunately this time --- talk. She said we were at a picnic in Japan and we were all sitting around a large picnic table. It was a unit party and there were a group of people sitting with our family. She said I looked around the table and pointed to each person stating, "I like "dat" face, "dat" face, "dat" face, and when I got to her face I said, "but I don't like that face." What did I mean and how had this been an incident which would scar her enough to remember it and tell me about when I was in my late teens. She had internalized it to mean I did not like her face because it was the only dark face. She said the picnic table was filled with people who were either Japanese or White. What did I know about this at two years old? Maybe she had given me a spanking that day or took a toy away, I don't know. Again, after hearing I did that I felt as though I was insensitive and a disappointment to her. I had hurt my mother and embarrassed her without a clue and it bothers me enough to remember just like she did. But again, "we" have caused heartache about color and hues and pigment. My mother had a reason to be sensitive. And this is why I say, "little dark skin girls who are continually "put down" by their own race because of the degree of pigment their skin has, "may" grow up thinking they are not beautiful. My mother had sensitivity, but she was one of the lucky ones --- she was beautiful and she never carried herself as though she thought she wasn't. She was the epitome of class, sophistication, and confidence. It was just those moments, when "old dark ghosts" came crashing inward.

Chapter III
"Brother Do You Mind"

We have created so many issues within our race. There is no more time to blame "the man". As long as we continue to blame "the man" for all of our problems, we will always have "second hand" lives. We will always get "their" hand me downs. We have to take responsibility for our lives and our own personal futures. We have to work on ourselves as individuals in order to make a stronger race of people. I try to tell my middle school students this everyday. When they are fighting amongst themselves, seven or eight children, boys or girls, or all genders together, are jumping on one child for no apparent reason, I blatantly tell them; stop talking about White people and how they don't like Black people." "In this day and age, White people are the last thing you have to worry about. You have to worry about those who look just like you." What stays on my mind is this young, Black girl telling me that she and three other girls beat up a young fat, girl walking home. I asked her why and she told me because it was fun. She talked about how the girl was begging them to stop, but that made them want to hit her more. We can not continue to scream racism when we are constantly racing against ourselves. Most of our Black parents seem to accept the behaviors of their children as normal.

My issues of late have been with Black men who become so angry when they see a "sista" dating or marrying someone outside our race. "Y'all" get really mad when it happens to be a "White guy". There is a deeper resentment when the man on the arm of a "sista" is White as opposed to Hispanic or some other more ethnic nationality. It has happened a million times. You pull up to a traffic light and there is a car occupied by Black men. The stares and angry looks are imminent. You know that you will get the look. I was eating at IHOP (The International House of Pancakes) one Sunday morning with a man, who at the time was my husband, as I stated earlier he happened to be White. After we ate breakfast, we went to the cashier to pay our bill. I turned around waiting for the cashier and some movement in the kitchen caught my eye. There was about three or four Black men with their cooking hats and gear on. They were staring a whole through me.

At first I thought that maybe they knew me or maybe my hair had a pancake in it or something, but when the guy in front of the others threw his hands up and said, "Why?" I knew the deal. Why was I with this White man and why was it **any of their business?** One late night after going out dancing, my husband, his brother and I went to eat at Crystal's. There was a young Black guy at the counter who became so angry at the site of me with them he began muttering comments under his breath while looking directly into my face. My husband became angry and wanted to retaliate, but his brother calmed him down. More recently, I went into the same place late one night with a Caucasian "friend". There was about eight or nine young Black men sitting down in an open area away from the counter. When we walked in they all stopped talking and watched us as if we were an Oscar award winning movie --- but one they didn't enjoy. This friend of mine is a very buff, bodybuilder who is not easily intimidated and often is the source of intimidation just because of his size, but they still did their sneers and looks of anger. My friend noticed it right away and has noticed it before. He told me of an instance when he was downtown in a nightclub hanging out with a friend. He said an attractive Black woman walked by hand in hand with a White guy, maybe her boyfriend, maybe her husband --- who knows; but he said a group of Black guys were standing close to him and when they saw the woman pass by with the White guy they grabbed her hand and said, "What's up?" If the situation had been reversed, if some White guys had grabbed the arm of a White woman walking with a Black guy --- think about it.

Another situation happened while I was working out at my neighborhood gym. I met this Black gentleman and every day I went to the gym he would compliment me and talk to me about various things while I was working out on various aerobic equipment. Sometimes I wanted him to be quiet because I don't like talking when I am working out (rather they are Black or White, let me make that clear). But I would talk and be as friendly as possible rather I was out of breath or not. One day, he saw me working out with a White guy who is a personal trainer. He and I were close and we had begun working out together. The Black gentleman approached me while I was by myself getting a drink of water from the water fountain. "Is that your trainer?" he asked. I answered, "Yes, he's a friend of mine and he's just helping me out a little." From that day forward this guy who had been talking to me for months stopped speaking and had an air of animosity towards me. I had done nothing, absolutely nothing to make him change.

And on top of this situation, there was the sweetest guy I thought I had ever met who also worked out at the gym. He was somewhat attractive, nice build and happened to be Black. He had a great personality. He always complimented me and told me how pretty I was or how good my workout was going. We talked and laughed all of the time. He invited me over to his house to watch a movie and have some wine. I contemplated going, but it was close to the holidays and I did not get the opportunity to visit him. In the mean time, he too saw me early one morning in the gym. The guy who was my friend and who had been helping me with my workout was there and again he happened to be White and the other guy, Black. He saw my friend, the trainer, talking to me. He saw him hug me and give me a kiss on my forehead. I felt the pressure and I almost wished he had not seen those things. But, here I go again, why should I care? The "Black" guy was not my boyfriend and I had never encouraged anything but friendship. That morning, in the gym, when I tried to make conversation he was very cold and distant. I asked him what was wrong and he said he didn't feel good. If he was so sick, why was he in the gym? It really hurt my feelings and made me feel as though I did something to betray him and I don't even know his last name. When I left the gym he was talking to a Black deputy sheriff who was also working out. This guy, the sheriff, had talked to me before and shown some interest in taking me out. He had made some comments about my choice in men to a friend of mine, but he is one of those "brothas" that has dated white women on many occasions and he was not always choosy about the ones he dated. Yet, he and the guy who claimed he was sick, gave me that once again "look." And I accepted it for the 100th time.

Generally these particular men appear to be uneducated people, but there are those times when you have some "brothas" who appear to be the opposite. They are educated professional Black men with degrees, fraternities, money, class, etc. and yet, they too will do "the look". "Brothas" it is time to get over it. Just mind your own business and I'll continue to mind mine. Stop taking this personal. It, "in my book", has nothing to do with you. It is my choice, period. I am around plenty of Black friends, you just don't **notice** during those times.

But, "many" Black men before the onset of the Black is Beautiful Movement and upon the decline of the Black is Beautiful Movement disregarded our ethnicity as beautiful and held us to the European standards of beauty probably because they were fed this notion of beauty for decades through the media (not to mention, as before, the damage slavery did in separating African-Americans by "house and by field".) But we are and can be an intellectual group of people. We can and should have shed these notions that were imposed upon us at a very different time and place. We now have possibilities and opportunities that some would never dream imaginable. I remember the times in the early 70s when my mother would yell to us to come look at television because there was a Black person on TV. We would drop whatever we were doing to see such a novelty. And now, there is nothing unusual about seeing us in magazines, movies, television shows, music video,etc. We have fought and loss blood to have the rights we should have always had. I have taken offense to things I have heard growing up. But most of the times it has been my own race that has been offensive and prejudiced. Black females were either telling me that I talked or acted too "white" (again as if the good standard English only belongs to one race). The fact that I did not speak Ebonics, in their eyes, made me less Black. And Black women, friends and foes, have ways been quick to tell "brothas", "don't waste your time talking her to her, she doesn't like Black men." Never once have I expressed this sentiment to anyone. I once heard a Black woman on a television show, I think Oprah, say she was not attracted to Black men and no matter how smart or good looking they were, she would never be interested. I am in no way a peer of hers. I would never exclude any human being. To dislike your race is to dislike yourself. I do not dislike my race or who I am, or where my roots originated.

But, what I do dislike is the behavior of a vast majority of my race and the ideologies which are expressed through their blatant behaviors. Comments that I have heard from male and female, young and old "turn me away" and make me appear aloof. When a Black man tells me or a friend outside in the parking lot of a predominantly African-American Junior College in Atlanta, where I have been studying African-American History, reading books such as "Before the Mayflower," "Hey, y'all come here, we like light skin women." I want to slap the taste out of his mouth. When I hear my dark skin friend tell me she was in a club and some "brothas" told her she was really pretty for a dark skin girl and then in turn asked her, "Do you have any light skinned friends?" I again would want to slap the taste out of their mouths. Some of this way of thinking and experiencing some of these situations may be what has caused me to date outside of my race competing with women in general, but not competing with the "color consciousness" of some Black men and all that goes with that. Never have I had a man of another race describe me as a redbone or make a distinction about the texture of my hair, or pick a part my features or talk about another friend of mine being too black.

I may have a light complexion, what some have called yellow or red bone, but I take offense to this fascination with pigment and hair texture. Just recently, a colleague I work with was at a barbecue my friend was giving. Being that I was not at work, I had my hair down as I usually wear it in a pony tail at work. I had on a white t-shirt that fell slightly off of the shoulders and a pair of fitted white jersey pants. Of course my attire was different than on the job. This educated man said, "Hey, you know you look good tonight. You look different than when you are at work. You should be able to get a lot of men because your hair is long and you have that light skin." What if I had one leg and I was long haired and light skinned? What if my face was scarred, but I was light skin? Do these qualities supercede everything? So, if I was exactly the same me, but several shades darker, I would not be attractive?

Just a couple of days ago, a White guy that I have been dating for about a year told me a Black man he works with said on the average Black women are not as clean as White women. I hate to even put this ignorance in writing, but I have to do it. He is probably the type of man no woman Black or White would ever even glance at, but the fact that he would speak so ugly against women that look like his mother makes me sick. Again, I would really like to slap the taste out of his mouth How can you generalize and make such an ignorant statement. What an IDIOT! Not only did he make this comment, but he made it to someone outside his race and yet if someone outside his race said it about his "mammy", he would want to fight and I would hope HE WOULD GET HIS ASS KICKED.

The scary thing is that these beliefs and ideology continue to grow. As we grow as a people, we are still perpetuating stupid myths and ignorant ideas of beauty. How do we educate the uneducated when some of the educated are still thinking ignorant. The children at the middle school where I work have really opened my eyes to the ignorance that does not lie dormant. This school is about 98% Black and the inter racial prejudice is amazing. Handed down from their parents and the parents of their parents, etc. These young black people state time and time again that dark skin is ugly. Sad.

CHAPTER IV

" Brotha Do You Mind?"

The old saying, "if the shoe fits, wear it", applies here. So black men, all of you need not wear these shoes. But there are some of you whose feet fit these shoes perfectly. **Brotha' do you mind?** Stop giving us "sistas" the ignorant stares, sneers, and comments when you see us with men outside of our race. I know that you feel that we are related to you, but really we are not your blood sisters. I mean you are not in our immediate family. I guess what I want you to understand is that we have never seen you at any family reunions and we really don't know who you are. So for me, when I was married and my husband happened to be White, your stares and glares and looks of anger were puzzling. I wonder why you get so angry because you don't know me. My real brother, you know the black man who shares the same mom and dad with me, never had a problem with my husband and supported our relationship. So why is it bothering you? I have seen more black men than I can count involved and married into relationships with women outside of their race, particularly white women. I have had White men and women tell me how much Black men love White women . To each his own taste, not necessarily race. Black men, "brothas" have been in the zone with white women ever since they "were allowed". Why? Has it been the forbidden fruit thing? Because we know for a long time this fruit was off limits. As African-American females during slavery, we were not off limits. This was extremely difficult for the broken and tattered slave families because the women were not their own in many ways. The African American slave had to despair at "their" women being taken and violated. And these were "their women" in every stretch of the imagination. But those days are gone. No longer are White women "off limits" (and neither are "we"). No longer are White slave owners raping and possessing Black women. No one just got off of a boat. If you see us with a white man, it is not because we have no choice. I really hate to be tough on my race, especially Black men, because over time they have had it difficult. If they are not rich athletes or movies stars or politicians, they often are looked down upon in our society. They are generally mistrusted and misunderstood.

There have been countless scenarios where Black males have been mistreated on and off camera solely because of the color of their skin. People often do not want to ride in elevators with the average Black man or people are quick to cross the street when facing an on walking Black male or several Black males. Store owners doubt their intentions to pay and ignorantly assume all Black males will steal or "hold them up". Having two sons who are of mixed heritage, but are obviously products of the Black race, I feel your pain.I have spent many sleepless nights since my sons became old enough to drive hoping and praying for their safety. I know that in the wrong place at the wrong time and even sometimes in the right place and the right time they could fall prey to racism. In our sister city of Columbus, Georgia a young, Black, professional male with a family was shot to death during a drug search. The officers thought the Black man driving an expensive SUV might possibly be a dope dealer. While lying on the ground with his hands behind his head, he was shot and killed. He was innocent... I feel this pain and injustice. I felt this injustice one early morning when my oldest son was arrested for walking in his girlfriend's neighborhood of predominantly White residents after 12:00 a.m. Yes, he had been drinking and he decided to walk home instead of drive. He was arrested and taken to jail in a city about thirty minutes from home. He was

31

not fighting or destroying property or selling drugs, but they whisked him away in the night --- some things will never change in deep, south Alabama, or the nation.

I felt the pain again when a teen-aged white girl obsessed with my younger son, stole into our house in the middle of the night and creeped into my son's room. She begged him to let her stay so that she would not get into trouble with her parents. When morning came and he tried to make her leave she became crazed and in a jealous rage. She began fighting with him and when he tried to push her out of the house she called the police who immediately handcuffed him and took him to jail with the threat of an assault charge even though he was in his own home. He was the "angry, Black male" and she was the sweet, little "white girl victim." My son was a popular student and very good baseball player with a future. She was a girl with little ambition and emotional issues. All she had to do is say, "he hit me," and it was done. When we went to court, everything was thrown out because I did my homework. I saved the crazy letters she wrote him and the pictures she tore up in his room and the e-mails, and the police report whereby she had stalked him at a party and keyed his car. But what if I had not protected my son, where would he be? He could possibly be where so many other young Black males have ended up --- behind doors that do not open from the inside. I saw a somewhat similar, but worse situation on Oprah. A young, Black athlete imprisoned because a young, white girl afraid of her father and her community cried "rape" over a young, Black male she was attracted to shows me the injustice of the Black males "walk down the road."

So, as always justifying myself to my race, I say this in order to say, do not consider me a traitor or an Uncle Tom or an "Oreo". I am just me and I am living my life the way I would choose to live it. I felt your pain before I ever had these two boys because I had a Black father and a Black brother. Both of these individuals have been upstanding in their own right. My father spent about 10 years in the Army, fought in the Korean war, transferred into the United States Air Force and spent about 15 years as a medic in this branch. My brother is presently a LTC in the United States Air Force. There are thousands of strong, intelligent, Black men all over the world and I acknowledge them every day. I have not dated or married outside of my race because I don't like my race or don't like Black men. I am a product of how I grew up. If I had grown up in a predominantly Asian culture, I probably would have been interested in Asian men and I don't rule them out.

Quite frankly and straight to the point, it is not even my non-cultural "upbringing" which has swayed my relationship behavior or taste. Once I "landed on Plymouth Rock" and experienced Black on Black racism, my focus changed and it conditioned what I would accept and what I would not accept. Men are men, hormones are not separated by color. Make no mistake, I do not think White men or any other race of men are better than Black men. That is not what this book is about. It is about the fact I care enough about Black men and my race to say, "Brother Do You Mind." If I did not care or give a damn about my race or heritage I would not be at the computer typing. I do care, I wish for change. I am not optimistic of a Black Renaissance. I do not think Black people will give up the color line and I do not think Black men will stop gaging our beauty by the degree of lightness, brightness, or whiteness or the texture of our hair.

African-American men have been pursuing and dating and marrying white women for years. Dating back to Sidney Portier, Sammy Davis Jr., through modern day actors, and countless athletes like Jim Brown and O.J. Simpson, Black men of status and wealth have often attained the Caucasian trophy wife. As I may have stated before, my mother was a beautiful dark-skinned woman. She had beautiful African American features which allured men of all races and an awesome hour glass figure which often settled the flow of traffic. Yet, I remember her disappointment and distant feeling of hurt when O.J. Simpson made a comment on a talk show about the female anatomy. He stated that women were not supposed to have big butts, but that their rear ends should be shaped on each side like tear drops. This in no way described the African-American buttocks. It also no longer describes the buttocks of the average American White woman, we're all "fine" now! Since the onset of Beyonce and Jennifer Lopez the beauty of the African American and Hispanic "buttocks" has been celebrated by the media and public. Now most women of all colors, especially Caucasian women, strive for healthier buttocks. No longer do they want the flat, tear drop buttocks that Mr. Orenthal spoke about.

CHAPTER V

I grew up as an air force child during a time when there were few Blacks in the Air Force which yielded few Black families which yielded few Black playmates. When my dad retired from the air force, we returned to Atlanta, Georgia. This was my birthplace, but had never been my home. Moving to Atlanta after having lived in places like Japan, Okinawa, The Philippines, Montana, Maine, etc., was a culture shock. Where I had lived, I knew no differences in people. At least, I did not know the differences were divided by race. I knew, of course, that my skin was brown, but again, why did that have to make me different. When I moved to Atlanta and began elementary school, I quickly learned that my features were not just different because I was me, but different because my "people" were different.

Who taught me this lesson first---no, it wasn't the "prejudiced southern whites of "Jawja". It was my newly found African-American peers. Upon entering school, I made friends with anyone who wanted to be friends with me. Truly, I never reached out to anyone person or race. Those in the classes willing to befriend the new Black girl who talked funny would quickly become my friends. I met two blonde haired, blue-eyed white girls, Kim and Karen, who would become my best friends and one Black girl in particular (I will call her Jenny). Jenny and I lived on the same street so we spent a great deal of playtime together and rode the same bus home everyday. Kim and Karen lived a small distance from me, but I spent many nights and weekends with them and their family. Why did I become so close to them? I couldn't tell you. In my eyes as a child, there was no connection to them other than they befriended me before any other students. My African-American friend Jenny and I would become close and distant as time would go by. There was always some underlying competition that I still see today amongst African-American women.

The problem with many of my new Black friends or peers was that they immediately wanted to know such things like, "Why do you talk funny?", "Why do you talk like your White?" When did speaking properly become only a white owned trait. If you talk too proper, you must think your White. To this day men, women, and children still ask that stupid question. Rather they are educated or not, they still ask, "Why do you talk like you're White?" "Why do you act like you're White?"

Things were fine in elementary school, until the Black students begin to resent my friendships with white students. I did not find my seat among those who shared my color, but found my seat **where one was vacant**. I had become good friends with a young Black girl my age.. It was nice because she lived down the street from me. We also began hanging out after school and spending the night with each other. We continued our friendship through high school and kept in touch periodically into early adulthood. However, there was always a sense of tension and rivalry with her. I never had this sense of tension with Kim or Karen.

I don't think that I was any better looking than she at this time, but as humble as I can try to be, I know I was more attractive once we got through puberty and into high school. We were both at that "in-between" stage during middle school when your head is a little bigger than your body and your teeth stick out. She was taller and more developed than I, and she had already begun teen acne although she was only about 11 when we met.. She was a medium tone, brown skinned girl with a big forehead just like me. I have never thought of myself as a yellow girl or a redbone, but I was often called that. I think because my mother was dark, my father light, and my brother medium toned, color was just not something I thought much about. We were all different colors in my family. I just did not see color like others may have. My skin color never mattered. I think it never mattered because we grew up in the military world of the Air Force around predominantly White people who never discussed the *shades* of color and the grades of hair. I never heard cousins or grandparents say things like, shut up with your ugly, Black self. I did not ever think about being lighter or darker than blacks or whites. I just knew that I was my daddy's little girl. But as time would pass, Black folks would let me know that being his little girl did not mean I would be sheltered from the stupidity and ignorance of some of "my" people.

In relation to the term African-American, I do prefer Black. Maybe I prefer Black because I just became so accustomed to this term. But there are "those Black people" who would, deem some Blacks, less Black because of life experiences, status, income, dialect, or bi-racialness. There are often harsh judgments and unfair ridicule by our counterparts, both men and women of color.

"Why do you talk white?" or "She thinks she is white." Children often said this t me in school, but even stationed in Germany with my husband, there were adult women (of color, of course) who told other friends of mine, they did not like me because, "She tries to swing her ponytail like a white girl."

The ignorance we can possess sometimes is so great. We put so much emphasis on non-sense. We can not progress because we constantly worry about the wrong things. We worry about skin tone. We worry about hair texture. We let outward appearance and genetics rule how we feel about each other. Based on the part of me that caused some Blacks to say I acted too "White", I tried to change and down play these things, but it didn't matter. I can remember my beautiful departed mother once said to me, while visiting in Germany after the birth of my first son, "stop trying to be accepted and stop caring about whether "they" like you or not." Because even in Germany, a land rich in culture and exciting things to see and learn, Black women were worried about rather or not I was swinging my ponytail too "White". I finally have reached this point. I don't care what other people think of me. I don't care one bit if I don't seem Black enough or if Blacks don't like who I marry or who I date. Black people are the very first to ask, "Are you mixed?" There have been occasional times when Whites have asked this question because they too sometimes get "caught up" in thinking most Blacks who talk educated or "proper" and are light complexioned may have Caucasian in them. They may ask out of curiosity, but Blacks ask so they can determine your loyalty to "Blackness".

CHAPTER VI

I often feel empathy for people like Tiger Woods or Mariah Carey who are inter-racial offsprings. Black people are quick to attack them and make them declare their Blackness. With Tiger Woods they were immediately obsessed with whether or not he thought he was Black. African-Americans, both ignorant and ignorantly educated, wanted to make him choose one heritage over the other. Why should he deny his Thai heritage in order to give more credence to the Black heritage. Why couldn't he just celebrate both because he is both. A friend once made the comment in another context, "two Chihuahuas don't make a Labrador". A Black man and a Thai woman do not produce a black offspring. They breed a child made from both races. And Blacks are constantly "sweating" Oprah Winfrey. Her crime is that she makes so much money and has "forgotten where she came from." She shouldn't have to justify her wealth or who she donates to, or how she tries to talk "so proper". We should be happy that we live in an era where a Black woman can be an "Oprah". Some black people may talk with an ethnic dialect which is cultural and many Hispanics talk also with cultural dialects as other nationalities of people, but do Hispanics place so much emphasis on how " white" some other Hispanic is talking or acting? When Chinese people see Connie Chung on the news, do they get mad or dislike her because she sounds and acts so "white" and also has "up" and married a White man? I have had educated Black people laugh or tease because my dialect was proper and sounded so "white". I hate to think that being educated is synonymous with being white. The English language is the English language, period. It doesn't have a color tagged on to it. Some of the children at my school quite naturally talk "Ebonics" and have asked me if I am part White. I think they ask me this because of the way I talk. Their dialect is so thick that one can barely determine if they are speaking another language. Unless they are comfortable or joking around with friends, when they speak to an adult they never make eye contact and talk in a low, monotone voice when asked questions. There is no confidence in their demeanor and they fight against those that do have confidence and are articulate. One young girl came to our school and the girls taunted her constantly. She was pretty girl with a California type, valley girl accent. She got punched in her nose so hard that it almost broke. The girl who punched her did not like her because, "she thinks she's cute and she tries to talk white." This was DeJavu for me! If I heard that phrase once in school, I heard it a million times. And the funny thing is these girls grow up to be women saying the same stupid comments.

There was a Black woman I befriended in Germany. My husband and her husband were in the same unit and had gone out to the field for some weeks. She and I would hang out together and shop together. I was pregnant at the time with what would be my first child. I will never forget this woman looking at a picture of my mother and saying to me, "Since your husband isn't Black, what if your baby comes out dark like your mother?" I looked into her very dark face and I wondered did she think this would be a curse. Was she cursed? At the not so ripe age of about 23, I could not comprehend a more stupid question. It equated with the man who made the comment to one of my best friends, who happened to be dark skinned and very pretty, "You are really a pretty woman to have dark skin, do you have any light skin friends?

Even recently, in the past ten years, working in a school environment with people who are supposed to be educated, I dealt with ignorance. And the ignorance that I dealt with was 98% from other Black people. Some of this focus is on who some might call lower economic, less educated Black Americans, but the sad truth is you can some times take the person out of the "country" or "ignorance", but you can't always take the "country" or "ignorance" out of the person. My point being I worked with people who may have grown up in a small town all of their lives, maybe, went away to school and majored in English or some other educational courses to actually teach young people knowledge and understanding of life and academics, and still maintained a small town, simple minded way of thinking. I actually had a principal at a middle school in the city where I was a counselor (Alabama), informed a new counselor to the area and to the high school about her new work environment and her new co-workers, this "educated" Black female described me (a counselor who cared about children and parents) as a Black woman with a Hispanic name, who was not Hispanic; but thinks she is White and is married to some poor White trash guy. I did not know this woman, at the time, from atom and believe me; she knew nothing about me. And she still doesn't. She teaches children and is a leader in an educational system. How about that?

I am so sick of Black people being fixated on the behaviors and personalities of other blacks who don't live up to what they feel is appropriate "Blackness or ethnicity." Some Blacks actually detested the Cosby show because they felt the actors "acted too White." As a Black person in general, I do not have an obligation to behave in any way which must be pleasing to others, Black or White. For so long, I have been so timid and intimidated to say how I really feel for fear that I won't be accepted or I would be misunderstood, or honestly that I wouldn't be perceived as Black enough. The people who talk in these ways about me, I finally realize, don't like themselves. Well guess what, I finally don't care. I am who I am.

CHAPTER VII
"Sista' Do You Mind"

Through all of the years that Black athletes have dated white trophy wives, little has been mentioned about their allegiance to their race or their chosen abstinence from "their own" black women. High fives, two snaps and a roll for the Black, famous athlete with the white, bleach blond wife and the millions of dollars. But I say, who cares what the athlete does or who he likes or loves. Again, he owes me nothing because I am a Black female. Many can argue that this is a slap in the face of the Black female because once the black male becomes famous his first major purchase after a Mercedes is a white woman. I have heard many Black women talk about how white women are "taking all of our men". As Iron Mike Tyson would say, "that's ludicrous". I haven't had a black woman, white woman, green or purple woman take away a man that loved me. You can't just look at a black man with a white woman and say she took one of your men. You don't even know this black man's name. He never was yours!

Why can't we find peace and harmony amongst each other as a people? Will we believe what Martin Luther king lived and died for to be truth and maybe have some rebirth and reawakening? No, probably not. No doubt during earlier decades African-Americans were discriminated in every way imaginable. Growing up as an air force dependent, my brother and I never knew that we were "supposed" to be different or "supposed" to be less than our white counterparts. However, when we returned to civilian life, which we had never known, we began seeing the clips and footage of the sixties when dogs were allowed to bite men, women, and children who only asked to be treated fairly. Who only asked to drink from a water fountain not labeled "colored only". People who only asked to live normal lives without having their husbands, fathers, sons, nephews, cousins, etc. lynched and mobbed in the middle of the night for any ridiculous reason. Maybe they sassed some white person in a store, maybe they stared at a white woman or girl for more than 3 seconds, whatever the reason, African-Americans have no doubt suffered because of the color of their skin. So how is it that we put ourselves through such prejudice --

-even to this day in 2006! It makes me sick. Working in a school mostly populated by African-American children you can still hear the prejudice and racism within the race being continually bred.

It is amazing working with young Black children in the middle school. They continue to perpetuate the myths that have been bred by ourselves for so long. These children tell me on a daily basis how ugly dark skin is. How can we continually fault Whites who we claim hate us when we hate ourselves. I debate with young African-American children every day trying to make them understand that the color of one's skin is not important. But further, I try to make them look beyond what they have learned about color from their parents. But then, who am I to tell them their parents are wrong.

White people adore their blonde, blue-eyed beauties, but you don't hear them speak with disgust of the brunettes or red heads within their race. How many times have ears of every race and color been in a supermarket or on the bus or just walking down the street and heard Black lips speak ignorance to a young child like, "get up with your ugly, black self." "Don't look at me with those big lips and your nappy head." Black people took the very features some of the white race tried to make ugly, through caricatures and television shows, and they perpetuated the myth that

Black is not beautiful. Yes, we have perpetuated are own selves as an ugly race.

Do all Black people do this? No, they do not, but so many do that it has become a cultural epidemic throughout generations. Dark skin is beautiful, all tones can be beautiful. One child told me that there are no unattractive light skinned people. Basically she is saying that all light skinned people are pretty. I wanted to walk her around the school and point out how untrue this was, but of course I could not do this. I wanted to take her to the mall on Saturday and just tell her to look around. All light skinned people are not tall, slim, model types. Generation after generation this ignorant way of thinking continues. Walking behind me or in front of me, at the mall, at the doctor's office, in the movie theater, wherever; I can hear a young, African-American parent as well as an older, mature parent yell out, "be quiet with your ugly, black self." It never stops.

More and more Black children are being born into an environment where by their own race does them much more harm than good. It is a verbal genocide of the mind. Parents are children's first teachers. They are impressionable and believe whatever we say to them. If we tell them they are stupid, they will become stupid. If we tell them they are good and they are smart, most times they will thrive and produce. If you water a plant and feed it, it will grow. If you sling mud on it, it will die. When we sling mud on our children by describing them as ugly, stupid, or dumb we stunt their ability to grow into positive human beings. And yet worse, when we put the adjective Black in front of these names, we destroy the essence of who they are and who they could become. I have yet to hear a White parent in a supermarket say, "Shut up with your ugly, white self." Sure, there are those parents who may be White; that can be just as abusive as any parent of any color. I have had to file complaints against many while working as a guidance counselor, but I have yet to hear them ever destroy their child by telling them the color of their skin makes them ugly or stupid. Why must "color" dominate everything we do?

In my very strong opinion, we do things to sometimes make ourselves an ugly race. We have the potential to be so many things inward and outward and yet we beat our own selves up with golden grills in our mouths, pants hanging off our butts, and hats cocked to the side. No, I am not really attracted to that. And then we have our women and young girls parading through the streets with red, green, and blue hair. Extensions do not bother me because White women have been wearing them for years. Beginning with Miss Kitty from Gunsmoke to Jessica Simpson, all women of any color will do things to enhance their beauty or lack of, but some of the things

African-American women have begun doing these last few years are ridiculous. Not only the multi-colored hair mentioned earlier, but the mounds of hair piled high on top of the head that looks like something you would store objects in. And it appears that there is some type of prestige associated with the height of these stupid hairdos. How can so many of us think this looks attractive. How can so many of us think that this coupled with pink house shoes and a gold or silver grill in our mouth looks good? Our young girls and (some of the not so young, should know better) parading through the streets with clothing so tight breasts and buttocks have no room to breathe. We know our anatomy and it is beautiful, but we don't have to accentuate what is already accentuated!

It is not only the physical we need to "tune up", but the attitudinal as well. I hate going into a place of business whether it is a burger place, retail store, or even a doctor's office (again with educated people) and have to wait to be addressed and then get "the look" and the smack of saliva hitting the roof of the tongue because you are too lazy to assist me while you are getting paid to do so. I don't know how many times I have had to wonder why some of my Black counterparts would ever work in an environment in which they would deal with the public. Make no mistake, I have had conflict with White people in the same settings because they did not either assist me properly or ignored me, but the general, stereotypical "two snaps and a roll Shaniqua" is prevalent. It is a "way" of mannerisms which make you feel as though this person of color just really doesn't like you. But, you know they don't know you.

CHAPTER VIII

I wish my thoughts and statements could be viewed with an open mind, but I already know the way my race works. I t will not be viewed in light of "what can we do to mend or make our race better." It will be looked upon as me disliking my race and that is not true. Most of my life, other Black people have looked at me from their own view, from their own firm, cultural biases and beliefs. We don't want White people to judge us based on ignorance or what their grandparents may have thought about Black people in the 60s. We want them to know that we are intelligent human beings with culture, morals, and beliefs. Albeit our experiences might be different from most Whites, or Latinos, or whomever, it doesn't make anyone's experiences and beliefs less credible. My life and my cultural experiences were not of my own choosing. I grew up in an Air Force family during the 60s and 70s in places remote where there were few people of my race. I grew up in an eclectic world and I am glad of it. My culture is not the typical African-American culture and sometimes that makes me sad, sometimes I feel that I missed out. But other times, knowing that I experienced life amongst Phillipinos in the Philippines, Japanese in Japan, Germans in Germany, Hawaiians in Hawaii, and also lived in the United States in such remote places like Maine and Montana, I am so happy for my multicultural self. It has cost me some heartache as I stated earlier. It cost me heartache when in return to the United States and moving to Georgia little Black children wanted to fight sometimes because I talked White, it cost some heartache sometimes when adult, Black women discussed my allegiance to my race behind my back and told Black men "Don't even talk to her, she doesn't like Black men." It cost me some heartache when Black boys in high school didn't think I acted Black enough, but at the same time they were always searching for the light skin girls with long hair. It caused me heartache when I heard comments from other Blacks about dark skin people and my mother was dark. It cost me heartache when in my adult life, people of my own race judge me on their limited perceptions of who they think I am, but never have taken the time to know who I really am. I was a daughter, I was a wife, I was a sister, I am a mother, and I am a child of God with red blood running through my veins. This blood is neither Black nor White; but it sustains me. In all of the years I have dated, not one man outside of my race has ever judged me by how light or dark my skin is, they have never made comments about my hair unless to give me a compliment; the texture did not matter. Never have they made comments about the darkness of my friends or foes; but most importantly ---- they liked or loved me for me, for me ---- there is nothing which feels better.